# *LIFE THROUGH A LENS*

Edited by

Natalie Nightingale

First published in Great Britain in 2002 by
*POETRY NOW*
Remus House,
Coltsfoot Drive,
Peterborough, PE2 9JX
Telephone (01733) 898101
Fax (01733) 313524

All Rights Reserved

*Copyright Contributors 2002*

HB ISBN 0 75432 818 X
SB ISBN 0 75432 819 8

# *FOREWORD*

Although we are a nation of poets we are accused of not reading poetry, or buying poetry books. After many years of listening to the incessant gripes of poetry publishers, I can only assume that the books they publish, in general, are books that most people do not want to read.

Poetry should not be obscure, introverted, and as cryptic as a crossword puzzle: it is the poet's duty to reach out and embrace the world.

The world owes the poet nothing and we should not be expected to dig and delve into a rambling discourse searching for some inner meaning.

The reason we write poetry (and almost all of us do) is because we want to communicate: an ideal; an idea; or a specific feeling. Poetry is as essential in communication, as a letter; a radio; a telephone, and the main criterion for selecting the poems in this anthology is very simple: they communicate.

# CONTENTS

|  |  |  |
|---|---|---|
| Dream Of Dreams | Alan Brunwin | 1 |
| Two White Dogs Sleeping | Stewart Gordon | 2 |
| The Wind Whispered | Burgess J Barrow | 3 |
| Once Upon A Time | Ron Matthews Jr | 4 |
| Dot Taylor | Edmund Saint George Mooney | 6 |
| Memories Of A Runner | Martin Boyle | 7 |
| Golden Moments - A Never-Ending List | Christina B Cox | 8 |
| A Lovely Interlude | Gloria Hargreaves | 9 |
| A Man And His Dog | J Aldred | 10 |
| Golden Jubilee | Doris B Prescott | 11 |
| I Miss Cornwall | Stuart Trevaskiss | 12 |
| The Cherry Tree | Amanda Bosson | 13 |
| Wedding In The Moonlight | Karen Rust | 14 |
| My Son Michael | Michelle Knight | 15 |
| Ton Plus | G Wright | 16 |
| And Fell Before The Rain | Sparky | 17 |
| First Sight | Leslie Fine | 18 |
| The Cruise | Edith Antrobus | 19 |
| Tunnel's Bright Light | Katie Johnson | 20 |
| Enduring Love | Barbara J Kerks | 21 |
| A New Life | Rosemary J Povey | 22 |
| A Special Moment | Brigid Smith | 24 |
| Poetic Justice | Beverley Ziles | 25 |
| Winter Scene | Anne Solti | 26 |
| Christmas Eve | Marcella Pellow | 27 |
| Winter's End | Frederick Seymour | 28 |
| Special Moments | Joe Waterman | 29 |
| Time Is Now! | R Bissett | 30 |
| Top Deck On A Lut Bus | Betty Lightfoot | 31 |
| My Hero | V Swarbrick | 32 |
| Mise En Scène | Edna Sarsfield | 33 |
| More | John Crowe | 34 |
| On The Beach | Daphne Bruce | 35 |
| In The Great Eye | Jane Phillimore | 36 |
| Before You Go | C S J Kugele | 37 |

| | | |
|---|---|---|
| Strangers In The Night | Channon Cornwallis | 38 |
| First Night Nerves | M A Challis | 39 |
| Baby Dear | Helen Barwood | 40 |
| Spanning The Miles | Mary Skelton | 41 |
| Moments | Ann Linney | 42 |
| Dear Barbara | Anne Davey | 43 |
| Scarlet Cascades | Brian Wardle | 44 |
| Holiday | Joyce Walker | 45 |
| Our Treasured Shore | S Kettlewell | 46 |
| New Year Firework Show | B G Clarke | 47 |
| Eleven, Eleven, Eleven | S J Robinson | 48 |
| Family Ties | Chris Bilton | 49 |
| Bonding | Corinne Lovell | 50 |
| Great Heart | C Gaskin | 51 |
| We Are Family | Andrei Dorian Gheorghe | 52 |
| Close Relatives, Blood Ties | Kathleen Mary Scatchard | 53 |
| A Certain Somebody Behind The Armchair | Gillian Fisher | 54 |
| Oh Brother | Mike Vukasinovic | 55 |
| Mrs Spruce - Highley | H Croston | 56 |
| Our Alfi | Robert James Lewis | 57 |
| Families | Paula M Puddephatt | 58 |
| A Friend Called Maureen | K N Fordham | 59 |
| Mum | Sylvia E Clark | 60 |
| My Memories | E Kathleen Jones | 61 |
| You're My Friend | Don Woods | 62 |
| Home And Away | Ann Weavers | 63 |
| Sights, Sounds And Smells Of Christmas Past | Linda White | 64 |
| Parental Love | D J Fenwick | 65 |
| Reflections | Denny | 66 |
| Loving Sisters' Togetherness | Hilary Jill Robson | 68 |
| A Tribute To My Mum | Dawn Moore | 69 |
| Circle Of Love | Gemini Cherry | 70 |
| Family Cries . . . | Anon | 71 |
| Neil | Kristina Howells | 72 |
| Who Gave You That Smile? | Vicky Stevens | 73 |
| Year On | Geof Farrar | 74 |

| | | |
|---|---|---|
| Loving Feeling | Nichole Jackman | 75 |
| Pushka | Jean Paisley | 76 |
| From One Shilling And Three Pence A Week | James Leonard Clough | 77 |
| Someone Who Means The World To Me | Shantel Faure | 78 |
| I Almost Didn't Have A Mum | P Edwards | 79 |
| Father Of The Fatherless | Ken Price | 80 |
| Helen Remembered | Roma Davies | 81 |
| Christmas Reflections | Geoffrey Woodhead | 82 |
| A Special Tree | Margaret Upson | 83 |
| Nana's Station | Jeanette Gaffney | 84 |
| Mayflower's Children | Patricia Hopkins | 85 |
| Valentine Revisited | C O Burnell | 86 |
| Peace | John Lee | 87 |
| Mellow Yellow | Sheila Walters | 88 |
| What's Happened | Mary Tickle | 89 |
| To Love | David A Bray | 90 |
| The Violin | Carole Andrews | 91 |
| The Best Things In Life Is I'm Different | Kezian Martin | 92 |
| My Hope | Patricia M Farbrother | 93 |
| Hogmanay Time | Humera Hanif | 94 |
| You | Jane Isaac | 96 |
| My Heart's Desire | J Hickman | 97 |
| Blind Date | B R Walker | 98 |
| Friends | Pamela Earl | 99 |
| Hers | Gladys C'Ailceta | 100 |
| Dark Nights | Lisa Keevan | 101 |
| Dreaming Out Of The Window | Rod Trott | 102 |
| Shiva's Love Song (For W H Auden And T) | Richard Bonfield | 103 |
| Memories In The Sky | Richard Turland | 104 |
| Insignificance | A Norton | 105 |
| The Presents | Peter Asher | 106 |
| Father's Day | S J Davidson | 107 |
| It's A New Dawn | Carole A Cleverdon | 108 |
| Hunting Holly | Gerard Wilson | 109 |

| | | |
|---|---|---|
| Missed | Helen Blackadder | 110 |
| The Homecoming | Meryl | 111 |
| The Earth Will Become A Paradise | M MacDonald-Murray | 112 |
| The Storm | Alex Branthwaite | 113 |
| Beachcomber | Chris Glassfield | 114 |
| Spring Chicks | Wendy Watkin | 115 |
| The Dawn | E J Sharman | 116 |
| An Clàrsach | Séamas M Ó Dálaigh | 117 |
| Forever Sweet | Helen Owen | 118 |
| Wake Up Old Fossil, Wake Up! | George Saurombe | 119 |

## DREAM OF DREAMS
*(I dedicate this poem in memory of my dear mum, Eileen Brunwin)*

Let me hold your hand and I will take you on a wonderful journey through my dream.
We can now both go on together over the highest and bluest of Blue Mountains that glitter with beams of sparkling riches.
Travel on still further in so much happiness of this freedom my dream is now giving to us. Hand in hand we can carry on through green fields with trees bearing golden leaves and flowers that shine the brilliant colours of a rainbow.
And on and on we both will travel, until we finally reach my special golden stream.
There in the glorious warmth and brightness of the midday sun, we can then hold our arms open wide, letting the slight and gentle breeze take us both high up into the freedom of the blue blue sky.
We now can see far away in the distance just a single cloud that has a silver lining, yes! It is meant for just you and I.
We both can look down and gaze into our future from the glorious reflections of my special golden stream,
which is somehow telling us that this journey we're travelling on, is only just the beginning of a very wonderful dream.
You can still travel on with me much further in my dream, to a world that is so gentle and warm.
And perhaps we might not go back, we could decide to stay in my dream of golden dreams, and find this wonderful dream we now travel in, will make our lives happily reborn.

*Alan Brunwin*

## TWO WHITE DOGS SLEEPING

The moonlight's streaming in,
Across the window sills,
And spills onto the kitchen floor,
Illuminates the room within,
Where two white dogs are sleeping.
A large bean bag serves as their bed,
Comfortable, round and brilliant red,
A setting sun upon a vinyl floor,
Becomes a bright red mandala.
The two white dogs turned silver now,
Are curled up together, yang and yin,
They do not stir, even though
They both know that I am standing there.
I open wide the kitchen door
And see the silver and the red,
The two dogs sleeping on their bed,
The yang and yin, the room within,
The moonlight still is streaming in,
And I survey this wondrous scene,
Just standing quietly by the door,
A peacefulness and calm that's quite serene,
The stillness at Earth's core.

**Stewart Gordon**

## THE WIND WHISPERED

The memories that forever dwell within
are those that are not forgotten.
They linger in the mind so bright
a beacon of rare fresh light.

The day Mother kissed your wounded knee
and softly muttered mercy me
then slowly wiped away a tear
soothing ointment she did smear

They stand out as a shining star
the distance there, are never far.
The moment of your first kiss
the reality of happy bliss.

The day you finally walked down the aisle
the world stood still and you smiled
today you were the movie star
the smiling faces near and far.

*Burgess J Barrow*

## ONCE UPON A TIME
*(To commemorate my wife, Jan, and I blessing and retaking our wedding vows on 30th September 2000 after 18 years of marriage)*

'Twas from Worm's Head didst first I espy thee,
in a time when love was furthest from my mind,
'pon a small peninsula that reach'd out twa' Bristolian Sea
unaware that my life history was marked, our destinies, signed . . .

O' rocky outcrop spawned feelings yet lost in 'nother world,
almost first whence should I cast eye 'pon giggly schoolgirl.

How couldst I know what history yet to come,
that one fair day when God decreed that we should become one,
and, as I now give thanks to who or whatever
that sought for happiness, ensuring thee to I should be, forever . . .

Whosoever decreed this love, who bestowed this mortal lover?
Who ensured my arrow of love lay deep upon and within her?
And who was it that brought her eyes to meet upon mine,
and have our hearts beat together, as one, for all time?

Oh I hasten to that misty memory once upon a time
for a rock where the spark of love became no longer benign;
Cradled somewhere in the dark depths of my head, your mind
'til God destined our paths should cross and bring us to now, our time!

'Tis a memory neither can barely recall but it dost last.
A glance, a chance, a glimpse of a memory somewhere in our past;
A time when our hearts should have become one!
Tho' now our love will survive till the dying of the sun . . .

Two memories hence since our sojourn in Wales,
our roads became a junction, other roads faded to insignificance, paled;
And brought us now to this day where we will celebrate our union,
and, at last, in the sight of God we can truly, become one.

Once upon a time, those days of pain, those days of laughter,
now, with the blessing of Jesus Christ,
    we can live happily ever after . . .

**Ron Matthews Jr**

## DOT TAYLOR

Slowly dilating, within a sunset,
Of yellow iris, a blacker pupil,

Tumbling down like love, mocking and vaulting,
Heel of Pegasus, living your freedom,

Folded, finger, flight, catching a blood thrust,
Madly throughout your God flying body:

You ram up dead cloud, tearing a tear out,
Shredding the corpses, of their wet maggots:

The air has you now, like a glove of gold,
An eye of the sun, pagan, pagan, bird.

*Edmund Saint George Mooney*

## MEMORIES OF A RUNNER

It was a cold grey wintry morning
When we gathered; some far from home
A group of runners about to start
A journey into the unknown.

As we progressed on our way
A church and houses passed with ease
My body flowing rhythmically
Then barren fields and leafless trees.

On we ran; endlessly on
My stride now heavy and vague my thoughts
Images blurred as in a dream
Eyes fixed ahead as salvation I sought.

Now fear was gone for there around me
My fellow runners to trust and love
Their warmth and strength would carry me on
And human frailness I'd rise above.

There was a bond, a tie so strong
A feeling that we suffered as one
On this long and lonely road
Tired aching limbs and miles to run.

So I remember a special time
When mind and body came together
To beat the pain and nagging doubts
And biting winds of March's weather.

It was a rare and precious moment
When peace descended and spirit did soar
For a beauty was touched so pure and true
To remain in the heart for evermore.

*Martin Boyle*

## GOLDEN MOMENTS - A NEVER-ENDING LIST

The green leaves of spring
As they are bursting forth
Snow-covered landscapes
Letters through the front door

Raindrops dripping down the windows
Whistling wind through the trees
Golden shades of autumn
Dances of falling leaves

Rising of the mighty ocean
Waves crashing to shore
High on the wing
The seagulls call

Bleating of newborn lambs
Out on green hills
Laughter of children
When Xmas stockings are filled

Bird chorus as dawn arises
Croaking frogs in the pool
Wildlife in countryside
Clowns acting the fool

Trickling of the gentle streams
Owls hooting after dark
Stars gazing down from the blackness
Children playing in the park

Graceful shadows of gliding swans
Boating upon a serene lake
Picnics in the summertime
With home-made cakes.

*Christina B Cox*

## A LOVELY INTERLUDE

It was so beautiful
In shades of beige and brown
Bright blue eyes gleaming
Long fur around the crown.

Like a statue it stared
And didn't move a hair
But for the rustle of the leaves
I wouldn't have known it was there.

I worried that it would fall
From its narrow perch
But it was filled with confidence
Watchful and alert.

It didn't stay for very long
About a half an hour
Its stillness held my gaze
Its beauty I can't erase.

I do not know from where it came
Or where it left for later
I know I watch for my furry friend
One of the gifts of nature.

***Gloria Hargreaves***

## A Man And His Dog

Behind a spiky clump of thistle
A silent whistle
And a dog runs left
Another blown signal
The dog, eyes bright
Swerves to the right.

The quiet commands
Of a man in a field
And the flock's gate is sealed
For the dog crouches, quivering
Until relaxed by another call.
Runs fast, runs low
Quick, quick, slow.

The man holds the gate
The dog drives on
The pinfold beckons
Another quiet call
Man and dog blend
The sheep are safely penned.

*J Aldred*

## GOLDEN JUBILEE

Sir Jeffery lives in our street
He's a knight I'm told,
He's going to be busy soon
For the young and old.
The Queen will organise him
He's used to Royal pun,
Many folk will pray a lot
And have a lot of fun.
Flags will be flying,
Show them if you're able,
Don't forget the jellies
And cakes for the table.

***Doris B Prescott***

# I MISS CORNWALL

How I miss Cornwall
My special true home
I lived there for six or seven years
In a quiet bustly market town
Called Helston where the
Whole town was dependant
On agriculture needs and tourism
And of course fishing industry from the sea,
Where fish and meat pasties,
Ginsters pies, Devenish, Blue Anchor
Inn ale, Newquay steam beer
Scrumpy Jack cider were the local delicacies.

Cornwall, yes, has some lovely
Countryside too around Helston
Itself, like Rhan Minor,
Cangwith, Coverack, Porthtowan,
Porthonstock, Mullion, with
Its lovely beachy coves.

Living in Cradley Heath,
West Midlands for sometime
I think about the good times
In Cornwall, because
It was a lot easier,
Especially with my family.
Oh, I wish I could live
In Cornwall again.

**Stuart Trevaskiss**

## THE CHERRY TREE

The snow sat on the cherry tree soft in the morning sky
And chaffinches of pink and red perched on the branches high.
And as I watched the morning sun melted the snow to ice,
And made the tree shine full of lights against the morning sky.
I'd never seen a tree so bright and watched the sparkling fairy lights.
For God had lit this Christmas tree, with nature's help he'd had a spree
And made a garden full of lights to celebrate this Christmas sight.
And birds from every family drank droplets from the cherry tree,
Which in the spring would change again and give soft cover from
                                                  the rain.
And standing there in blossom pink, would stop and make us stand
And think of what a wonder nature is to give us sights as great as this.

*Amanda Bosson*

## WEDDING IN THE MOONLIGHT

Wedding in the moonlight
where the stars are shining bright
Gathered round are our family crowds
To watch us take those special vows.

We shall grow old together
no one shall come between us ever
I love you so much baby, can't you see
let's go off into that land of fantasy.

Baby, I hope this ring will help you see
your love really means everything to me
Watch the crowds as they dance
I think it's time to make romance.

*Karen Rust*

## MY SON MICHAEL

My special moment was
the day I gave birth to my
beautiful first born son Michael
it was the happiest day of my life
my very own baby boy
it was just what I always wanted
my little treasure was born at
City Hospital, Winson Green, Birmingham
at 1.30am was when he was born
he only weighed 4lb 15ozs
they say he looks like me but
I don't mind
he has just started to learn
how to walk it's quite funny
to watch him because when
you try to get him to walk
he starts to wiggle his bum
he looks like he's trying to walk
and dance at the same time
I wouldn't change him for the world
I love my son Michael
he's also started talking now
he says 'mamma', 'dada', 'nana' and 'no'
he is my gorgeous little boy
I'm just proud to have him
if it wasn't for the staff thinking
so quick then he wouldn't be
here with me today
my special moment
my son Michael.

*Michelle Knight*

## TON PLUS

Dull misty day, rain hung in the air
But, in our youth, we just had to be there.
At that station field near Tamworth,
Notebooks and pencils ready, as steam left this earth.

Rosy, myself, and a name long since gone,
Sheltered under the arch as the rain carried on,
A miserable day as September drew in
The first signs of winter that chill the skin.

A mournful wail from across the moor
Signalled a train, the rain continued to pour,
A whistle shrieked its warning sound
Above the sound of wheels spinning around.

'Neath the dark, heavy sky, sounds carried clear,
The express pounded on, it was getting near.
With a whoosh of steam she sped into sight,
As she cleared the bridge we stepped back in fright.

Monster machine bellowing steam and smoke,
She went by so fast, not one of us spoke,
Carriages streamed by until the red tail lamp
Disappeared in the murk of smoke and damp.

For years I had watched the trains pass by
At Tamworth Fields until steam had to die,
But, only once in those years in the sun
Had I witnessed steam doing the ton.

The rain carried on as I mounted my bike
And Rosy and me left the field to Mike,
It's all gone now, diesels cause no fuss,
Like the down Caledonian doing 100 plus.

*G Wright*

## AND FELL BEFORE THE RAIN

I heard your voice before my birth
Before I drew first breath
Your words like dreams came from the earth
On streams that surpassed death

And never will I turn from you
You draw me to your flame
Forever burning realms of blue
Where freedom calls your name

Your kingdom lies in sacred ground
Where everything can be
Immersed in beauty ancient sound
Eternal harmony

And nothing throws us to the sea
That drowned us in illusion
For something tells me here I'm free
No more is there confusion

So if I fall into the sun
Or work against the breeze
Remember when it all was one
The oceans and the trees

Remember how the time did run
Across the planet's floor
And so much damage soon was done
We cried out for the Evermore

So should I turn before the tide
And see it all again
Remember that a Martyr died
And fell before the Rain

*Sparky*

## FIRST SIGHT
*(A Victorian style poem of love)*

He walked the downs this sunny day
in awe of so much beauty seen.
Stopped in his tracks he stood amazed
as he saw her calmly reposed.

She lay amidst tall blowing grass,
sat up in fear at his approach.
The loveliest person he had seen,
that drained all breath from his being.

The words she spoke were velvet soft.
'You startled me' she spoke in shock.
Her deep brown eyes compelled one's stare
as did fair hair that freely flowed.

With skin so smooth that did deny
the years on earth that had been spent.
First youth which must have passed her by
not leaving usual trace behind.

He raised her gently there to stand.
Displaying figure of delight.
'I can't think why I was afeared'
rang silken words of gratitude.

There shone within this glowing warmth
that deemed to understand all things.
No bitterness or malice dwelled
with only goodness recognized.

Could love on sight he comprehend?
It now captured his whole being.
Her nature was transposed in him.
This being of pure rarity.

**Leslie Fine**

## THE CRUISE

A special moment in my life,
Was when I wasn't just a wife,
No household tasks, no Monday blues,
Just setting off for a heavenly cruise.
All my life I'd loved the ocean,
Just looking from the shore,
But this was an adventure,
I couldn't ask for more.
The company, the changing faces,
Those trips to all those far-off places,
The sun, the sands, the endless sea,
This is what life was meant to be.
The swimming, dancing, time for leisure,
Gave us both such endless pleasure,
But we felt it wasn't real,
That's what gave it such appeal.
They can't take away the memories,
Of these very special days,
They're locked away for ever,
In so very many ways.

**Edith Antrobus**

## TUNNEL'S BRIGHT LIGHT

It's summer in the air, but spring in the heart,
Now is the birth of the positive start.
As I look into the valley in the evening light,
I feel the sensation of fulfilment bite.
My enthusiasm erupts like a volcanic stream,
Gone is the want for the impossible dream.
The personality that was buried in the depths of the mind,
Is set free from the suffocating depression vine.

My senses are aroused by the natural call,
The birds, the trees, the summer rainfall.
Things that have been there for all of my days,
Until now was only background haze.
Now I'm back and I'm ready to feel,
Only now does the appreciation feel so real.

So I'm here, I'm now and I'm back to stay,
I'll steamroller depression if it gets in my way.
Take heed of the warning, never sit and whine,
Remember the sound of the happiness chime.

*Katie Johnson*

## ENDURING LOVE

Last Tuesday, sorting
Through old photographs,
I found one of you
As you were, not
As you are now. You,
Before children, the mortgage,
And a life that has driven
Your spark away.
You were so fresh
And precious and I
Remembered how it was
When we only had
Each other and the world
Was another's business.
I looked again and saw
Your eyes, the same eyes
That shine beneath
Your worried brow
Every morning as you
Kiss me at the door.
And in that moment
I realised your love
Was still as strong
And pure as before
We entered our years
Of marriage. And in that
Same moment, that special,
Special moment, I fell
In love with you again.

*Barbara J Kerks*

## A NEW LIFE

It's begun,
I'm scared.
My husband beside me,
He says it's shared.

Take it easy,
Don't worry.
You get the car,
Forget the curry.

Have I packed
What I shall need?
Ring my mum,
Now don't you speed.

The friendly smile,
The knowing wink.
It's amazing,
How far you sink.

You blame yourself,
You blame him.
Why did we do it?
I must have been dim.

Pressure, noise,
And now relax.
Send the news,
Out on the fax.

It seems like hours,
Since first we came.
It never was,
A gentle game.

I don't feel tired,
I should I know.
There's only that
Especial glow.

I've done it.
No it was two.
That little one here.
For me and you.

***Rosemary J Povey***

## A SPECIAL MOMENT

The evening light added a certain
Enhancement to the place,
As our coach finished
Its ascent, up the winding road.
My fellow travellers and I
Now entering the confines
Of Monte Cassino Abbey.
This was my special moment,
To be in this place of tranquillity,
Serenity, like a world apart.
Being in the church which
Is the custodian of Benedict's tomb,
Illustrious founder of this place,
Was a moment special, rare indeed.
A place in which to linger
And have a longer stay,
So I hope that some future itinerary
Will take me up the winding road,
Back to Monte Cassino
Some day.

*Brigid Smith*

## POETIC JUSTICE

A funny thing happened to me last night
When my sister came to visit.
We were talking about me writing poetry
I said I didn't think I could do it.
I've been doing it for years, you see
But never thought that they were that good.
Writing about people, situations and family
Depending on my mood.
But my sister said I should have a go
And I agreed to try.
Then the next day while looking through the paper,
Your advert caught my eye.
Was it a coincidence or fate?
I don't know what it could be.
I do know it made me write to you
What your response will be, I'll have to wait and see.

*Beverley Ziles*

## WINTER SCENE

I stood upon the hill,
pinnacle of the Sussex Downs.
My eye beheld the winter browns,
bare earth not fields
waiting expectant to be ploughed.

The neat framework of hedges
dividing precious soil like patchwork.
Painted farmland in variable shades of umber
and there beyond the silent scene
save seagulls, white against dark,
the village, made obvious by surrounding solitude.

Cottages huddling together for warmth
Smoke from a lone chimney
spiralling into dark damp air.
Church spire defying centuries of change.
Lighted windows betraying life within.
Darkness settling over the countryside.

The occasional sound of roosting pheasants.
Rabbits skipping, running, watchful, eating.
Foxes making plans in unseen dens.
Homeward I thread my way
through night's black cloak
rejoicing that I stood upon the hill
pinnacle of the Sussex Downs.

*Anne Solti*

## CHRISTMAS EVE

Midnight Mass
   on Christmas Eve
Our lovely church
   with candles glowing,
And all around
The presence of the Higher Power.

Our special priest
   our Man of God -
Led us through trials and stress
   to welcome once again
God's greatest gift -
   His Son
Lying so lowly in the manger.

Slowly, quietly
   we took The Host
The Holy Ghost
   brooding all around.

*Marcella Pellow*

## WINTER'S END

I stand
Within the shadow of my church
Sheltered from the cold hilltop wind.
I stay awhile to look upon.
What these lofty consecrated walls and windows see.
At present time a winter scene.

Christmas carols, sweet words of praise
In our hearts, and mind, linger on.
But for a while, the words, have gone.
Now the biting wing sings its winter's song.

Shimmering, frost covered fields.
Encompass distant farms.
Horses clad in winter coats.
Pull on frozen grass.
Red checked stable girls, in woollen gloves and scarf.
Trample frozen fields, with bags of treasured oats.

Through heavy winter clouds, faint rays of sun.
Can shed no warmth against the winter cold.
Trees, and woods are bare.
Until the sun is strong and bold.
This coming spring.

Spring is not far away.
For now the sun appears
Then fades, behind slow moving clouds.
Its rays of light, come and go.
Within the church.
It plays upon the warm translucent colours of the cross.
Blues and reds adorn the walls, and singing choir
Winter's soon to pass.

*Frederick Seymour*

## SPECIAL MOMENTS

I smell the flowers better than you and
hear the birds sing and feel the morning dew.
I feel the texture of cloth with a more sensitive hand
and when I walk the beach I can feel each grain of sand.
I hear the sigh of the wind in the trees that you don't hear,
but when I mention them you're hesitant and unclear.
I point these out but don't mean to be unkind, the only
reason that I notice them is because, you see, I'm blind.

*Joe Waterman*

# TIME IS NOW!

Often passing, ne'er a thought!
Invisible to naked eye;
If lost, cannot be ever caught,
Between our birth and day we die!

Used well, so much can be achieved,
Yet sadly, oft we squander;
Its use, is hopefully perceived,
As gaining life - much fonder!

Such waste, of thing so very rare!
Must cause great loss to every mind;
Forever after, searching where,
This priceless jewel we'll find!

Regret, o'er things we've left undone,
Can ruin a fruitful day;
Thus 'do it now' beneath the sun,
Is much the better way!

Deep thought, absorbs the very wise,
In learning when and how;
To capture such a worthy prize
And find that - time is now!

*R Bissett*

## TOP DECK ON A LUT BUS

I was nine and a bit
When I actually managed to sit
Top deck, on a LUT bus.
In those days kids like us
Cut their milk teeth on recycling
Toffee rationing and biking.

In those days if we dared answer back
Dads usually gave kids a crack
Or mams doled out back handers
The obvious propaganda
Such as 'speak when spoken to'
Was what grown-up people told you.

Between Asian flu and smogged-up noses
Childhood was no bed of roses.
In fact, in those days kids like us
Always stood when boarding a bus.
I was, I suppose, programmed to sit
On a LUT bus from nine and a bit.

Although LUT buses have moved on,
Because time and tide wait for no one
Imagine what kids today would say
If Blair announced today
They would be programmed to sit
Top deck, on a bus, from nine and a bit?

*Betty Lightfoot*

## MY HERO

All my life, I've seen you,
In a very special way.
For you have been my hero,
Through all my childhood days.
As I watched you fix and mend,
Like all good fathers do.
I stood and gazed in wonder,
As you made my dreams come true.
For you have always been,
A man so strong and true.
With never any thoughts,
To the hardship you've been through.
How can I ever thank you,
For the love you've given me.
For you have been my guidance,
You've shown how good life can be.

*V Swarbrick*

## MISE EN SCÈNE

The taste,
long forgotten
on the tongue,
lay sapient.
Perception waited.
Mischievous, wicked
thoughts, begin to form.
Pulsing with discovery,
barbed tangs of honeyed
sweetness, salivate in
anticipation.
Chimerical imaginary reaches
the once dry lips,
au courant, posted
in the picture.
Words, no longer random,
articulate,
my after dinner speech
had begun.

*Edna Sarsfield*

## MORE

'You *already* give me joy'
She said
And *meant* it

Fine
Except
That opportunity to give more joy
Was missed
For
What are a few extra moments
In bed
As opposed to those in the bath
Except as missed opportunity
To give her a little more joy?
And I say that I'm not selfish
What a laugh!
But
The lesson of all this
I shall not miss -
Always take every opportunity
To give other
*More* bliss!

*John Crowe*

## ON THE BEACH

The languid sea is dozing in the heat
It idly rolls wet pebbles to and fro.
Like liquid flesh around this fiery globe
It waits, a brooding bride, for pagan wind.
Together soon, they'll whirl in wildest dance
And shout tumultuous psalms to moon and sun.
The earth spins on. It seethes with life
Whose hymn of love has only just begun.

*Daphne Bruce*

## IN THE GREAT EYE

Oh, you great eye
Up in the sky
How hard we try
To float and fly
Before we die

Oh wheel, go round
And spin the ground
Until we've found
Great London town
Turned upside down

Oh, you great eye
Up in the sky
Please help us try
To float and fly
Before we die.

*Jane Phillimore*

## BEFORE YOU GO

Before you go,
Look upon this garden,
Remembering each tree, each vista, every lovely rose.
Linger pensively in this paradise a moment longer than the last moment
Before you go.

Before you go,
Stand within this house,
Remembering each face, each voice, every fond embrace.
Linger wistfully within these walls a moment longer than the
                                        last moment
Before you go.

*C S J Kugele*

## STRANGERS IN THE NIGHT

I was at a friend's reception when I looked across the room to see
a stranger standing mesmerised and mesmerised by me!
Our eyes looked and he smiled a smile that made my knees go weak
but to look mature, I broke the stare, we never got to speak.
All night he followed me around, just standing out of range,
my cheeks were pink, embarrassed? Yes, the situation was so strange.
It's said there's a partner for everyone, you get just one chance to find,
it was more than just a sensation, I felt this man lived in my mind.
Wherever I walked round that evening those soft eyes
                     were watching me go,
but I wouldn't maintain the eye contact as this man was
                     a stranger you know.
I was not there alone and neither was he but I did ask if he
                     were a guest?
My escort replied he was an unknown and not recognised by the rest.
So even to the gathering a stranger he was just passing
                     time there that night.
With the party being a long way from my home to introduce
                     myself didn't seem right.
I'd love to say we met again, but no, it didn't happen
but I wonder often about that night when sitting on my own
the girl he was with could have just been a close friend?
He could really have been my own special Mr Right,
but we parted without a single word being spoken
two ships that just passed enchanted in the night.

*Channon Cornwallis*

## FIRST NIGHT NERVES

So small, and so very delicate,
I fear that she might break.
The longing to hold my baby is there,
but how my hands shake.

Two hours old,
she already has a mop of hair.
My heart is more than willing,
to show her how much I care.

Butterflies in my stomach,
I approach at snail's pace.
What if these arms should drop her?
My pulse begins to race.

Looking down at her,
the fear suddenly fades away.
My heart has been waiting,
for this very special day.

Cradled in my arms,
her head resting on my chest.
My eyes wide open with wonder,
knowing that my life has been blessed.

It feels so very natural,
holding my baby daughter tight.
In my soul I will always cherish,
this very special night.

*M A Challis*

## BABY DEAR

The angels sent you from above,
For me to cherish and to love,
With tiny fingers and tiny toes,
Rosebud lips and a turned up nose,
Big blue eyes and flaxen curls,
You are a beautiful baby girl,
May angels watch over your cradle each night,
Keeping you safe till morning light.

*Helen Barwood*

## SPANNING THE MILES

Hand touching hand
   touching cheek -
      caressing.
This is God's strength
   giving each
      heavenly blessing -
For our Lord never fails
   to make Himself known
in our weakest of moments
   when we feel so alone -
And my hand touches
   'your' hand
With a love that's so
   true -
As the light of our world
reveals His presence to you.

***Mary Skelton***

## MOMENTS

There have been so many special moments in my life,
So many sights to see and sounds to hear.
I lock them safely in my memory
To bring out later and enjoy again.

I can recall my wedding day so many years ago;
My new-born babies' cries, their first smiles and
Their faltering steps, their little hands in mine,
The day they first called me 'Mummy', their first kiss too.

A glorious sunset on a summer's eve,
The sky and earth bathed in a golden hue,
And after, the deep violet night
With bright stars twinkling in the void above.

A winter storm upon a Cornish beach
With huge waves crashing loudly 'gainst the cliffs;
The white spray flying high into the air
And seagulls wheeling in the treacherous wind.

I see a skylark rising from the ground
And hear its wondrous song as it flies up;
And watch the buzzards soaring round the tor
Mewing like kittens in the moorland air.

The special moment when we have just performed
A grand musical opus with a choir;
Great waves of sound that echo round my head
And fill my heart with happiness and joy.

These precious moments in my memory
Are mine to keep and think on when I may;
So many special moments to recall
That have enriched my life along the way.

*Ann Linney*

## DEAR BARBARA

Dear Barbara,
    Oh Barbara, sorry I phoned you today
    It really upset me in what you had to say
    Not knowing your dad had passed away
    Now in God's loving care, he's on his way
    Christmas time for you won't be much fun
    Your dad will give you strength for what you've done
    I know your heart is broken, and you're very sad
    But now at least there is peace for your dad
    I know what you are going through, trust me I know
    Losing someone so close to you, is such a heavy blow
    When Christmas is all over, then you can rest
    Barbara try to put things behind you and give it your best
    I am your friend and always there for you
    I can feel your sadness, knowing what I went through
    Why the Lord takes the good ones, I will never know
    So now you feel bitter about this, please let it go
    Try to face the future with a smile.

        God bless you dear friend
        In your hours of sadness
        Thinking of you always
              Anne XXX

*Anne Davey*

## SCARLET CASCADES

Her face told the wonders
Of the falling snowflake
Or three snowy white swans
On a crystal blue lake
I held her hand gently
As life starts to fade
Stroked her hair down the pillow
In a scarlet cascade
While the angels sang softly
I kissed her goodbye
Then they carried her off
To eternal love beyond the sky.
Now my heart holds fond memories
With each falling snowflake
Or three snowy white swans
On the crystal blue lake
The tears on my pillow
Which my memories have made
Can't wash out the colours
Of her scarlet cascade.

*Brian Wardle*

## HOLIDAY

Train ticket lost,
More extra cost.
Lie on my bed,
Drinks go to my head.
Days never fair,
Just rain, I don't care.
The holiday's come
I'm going to have fun.

*Joyce Walker*

## OUR TREASURED SHORE

It was a wonderful holiday,
the sea's orchestral manoeuvres
entwined with the skylarks' morn song
sent rapture through my whole body.
Every morn stood on the clifftop
as the sun rose to bless the land,
such euphoric splendour abound.

'Twas a good time then.
No cares, no forlorn illusions to caress,
just sweet harmony upon our day,
the golden sands which pass not as time
still lie in placid rest.
Kissing still - the ripples of the seas
as the tern hovers to glide.

Two hearts in oblivion of times trespass,
sweet whispers of the sea breeze.
Oh to fly free again my love like then.
The sun shone so radiant amid your curls
golden, liken to silk never seen.
Your tender voice like a dove mellow
still rings amid my harkening ear.

Still, what life shall be but emptiness
if your pathway was but away from me.
Thus shall fate be but kindness
for us to share our every morrow,
the child born this sacred dawn
shall rise in glory to walk there.
Then, shall we my love again, embrace
together our treasured shore.

*S Kettlewell*

## NEW YEAR FIREWORK SHOW

Coldest time of year; again.
Celebrating warm friendship.
With old and new friends
Seeing the old year out;
Greeting the new year in, at midnight turnabout.

Firework party show,
To a backcloth of snow.
Colourful arcs of sparkling glows.
Roman candles, popping rainbow coloured balls.
Reflected in white snow, pretty shooting balls.

Fire fountainheads, spouting bright flames.
Dozens of fireworks, all the same.
Brightly imitating silver rain.
Sky rockets, skyward bound.
Busting stars, way above the ground.

Glowing lights, falling starlets drop.
With bangs and pops.
Above the newly snow covered rooftops
Mirrored on snow; mirror white ground.
Hundreds of pounds worth of firework colours rebound.

Standing in the snow, shaking hands.
With this world, Anne's and Dan's.
Singing 'Auld Lang Syne' to accompaniment of the band.
Waving goodbye, God bless you
To friends old and new, special moments;
Happy New Year to you.

*B G Clarke*

## ELEVEN, ELEVEN, ELEVEN

I woke and it was morning
The guns at last were dead
An Armistice, signed yesterday
Has chased away that dread

The nurses all were smiling,
The lads were giving cheers
As great news of that signing
Still rang about their ears.

Eleven, eleven, eleven!
It should be wrought in song.
Eleven, eleven, eleven
That moment sought for long.

*S J Robinson*

## FAMILY TIES

*Age, Two Minutes*

Stolen streets I walk, angular in thought,
Tip-toeing through turbulent emotions,
To be born is no easy journey, but what do I know?
And domesticity will be overturned.

She is now here, struggle and sleep, my girl.
You lay before me, a sentient being, here forever.
Will you read books? I am driven to observe,
Be neat in all things, watchers beyond the walls see all.

A cap of steel clamps the mind, to know the future,
Not in an obvious way, but confined to life's periphery,
And chance meetings cannot be extinguished,
Recycle your thoughts through a prism, do not shirk.

Solemn, your eyes, look into mine with recognition,
See me, yes me your father, you are platinum,
You are the shiniest thing in the shop,
Learn laughter in your heart, as your mother did.

***Chris Bilton***

## BONDING

Loving relationships,
Close family bonds,
Need lots of nourishment
Not magic wands.
Remembering things that
My own mother said,
At the time I thought, rubbish,
But not now she's dead.
You find yourself passing
Them on to your young,
And then they tell their kids
And so it goes on . . .
Family ties are quite
Hard to define,
You make them, don't break them;
I'm working on mine!

*Corinne Lovell*

## GREAT HEART

Nigh on sixty years ago I met him
In India's one time capital Calcutta.
He from Malaysia's Singapore had come
And just laughed at sight of fellow airman -
Dishevelled and unshaven, having travelled
From England via the Cape, by sea and train.
Five months it took; five months of deprivation,
When to be clean was quite exceptional.
our Lady's Church our rendezvous became;
Where we discovered strengths and peccadilloes.
In Darjeeling next on tea plantation
Under Himalayan peaks we rested.
Both in Quetta's hospital together
Recovered from pneumonia or such,
And later roamed the North West's arid hills.
By chance it was near Mandalay we met.
And in Rangoon our paths crossed once again.
Always he smoked, he talked, he laughed, he cared.
Of war's companions truly he was friend.
With peace he went back to his Scottish home,
Near Bannockburn the site of English dead,
And settled there to teacher's wedded life.
They were not long those happy years they shared -
Time ended close on forty years ago.
Love knows it not; is blind to all; sees but
A family that share a mutual pride.
My privilege to peep behind that veil
For friendship's warmth survives the cold of death.
My joy to share my vision, sketched with care,
And proudly done; nor would I be denied
The seal of friendship's giving of oneself.
Tommy McFarlane thank you and God bless.

*C Gaskin*

## WE ARE FAMILY
*(Post Christmas Reflection)*

What was the star of the kings,
heralding our Saviour?
A supernova? A Comet?
Some fireballs repeating the same way?
A conjunction between two heavenly bodies,
surrounded by divinity?
Who knows . . ?

The star of the kings
changed the order of the things in the sky,
lowering heaven into our human souls.
But only understanding and accepting this,
we become a part of
the astral family.

**Andrei Dorian Gheorghe**

## CLOSE RELATIVES, BLOOD TIES

Who gave so much without thought of reward,
Who cared and shared the childhood tears and joys,
Then sympathised with all the dreams we'd stored,
As hearts got broken like our favourite toys.

We changed and grew, we reached maturity,
Yet never outgrew love which never ends,
Families trusted in sincerity,
Family still, but also loving friends.

Parents whose wisdom reached us down the years,
Children whose freedom did not us exclude,
Happiness shared, also sorrow and fears,
A future hoped for through this first prelude.

How can our gratitude be adequate,
For health and education in your care,
Hope these few words serve to appreciate,
Your love, thank you dear ones for being there.

**Kathleen Mary Scatchard**

## A CERTAIN SOMEBODY BEHIND THE ARMCHAIR

Had a last minute walk in her spaniel-skull mind.
The lead hung through her mouth. She dropped a canine hint -
Some breaths of the night air before she was confined

By locked doors for hours. I swear I saw a glint
Of pleading in her cocker eyes, when a paw came
On my arm. For nothing would she miss a late stint.

There could be puddles on the way. She loved her game
Of 'muddy fur's fun, but wetter is better'.
Though I thought Honey had been given the wrong name -
It wouldn't have suited a romping red setter.

*Gillian Fisher*

## OH BROTHER

When I think of all the times
You cared for me
I want to curl up
On your ragged floor
I talk of the times when you grew up
All from the cup
I bow at your wisdom
And chose to come
To see me again
Will your daughter
I ask only to be a part
Of your heart.

*Mike Vukasinovic*

## MRS SPRUCE - HIGHLEY
*(From a very grateful evacuee - Highley 1941-1945 - Buddy)*

This lady was and will always be,
A constant reminder of my integrity,
Who through my war years as a child,
Gave her love through a smile!

She baked the most fantastic cakes,
Full of cream, they were just great,
She had a charm all of her own,
Just like her home baked scones.

I always am, I will always be,
Indebted to this fine lady,
I can't deny it, there's no excuse,
There's only one Mrs Spruce!

**H Croston**

## OUR ALFI

Our Alfi he is special
He keeps us together night and day
He might be our dog but he is clever
He is always there when we are down
He is always there when things don't go well,
Alfi comes on protests to save his brother and sisters
From the day we got him when he was small
To a grown dog he is still our Alfi
He never lets us down
That is why Alfi is so special to us.

*Robert James Lewis*

## FAMILIES

It would be great fun to invent your
own ideal
family; pure
indulgence.

You choose your friends. Even then you make mistakes.

Perhaps one could invent a
virtual family? What an opportunity
that would be: A
lovely fantasy . . .

How strange it is to think this way. You wouldn't then
be you.

***Paula M Puddephatt***

## A Friend Called Maureen

The path of life is never smooth,
It twists and turns all ways,
But the people we encounter there,
Can brighten up our days.

There are some special people,
The ones that we call friends,
Who ask for nothing in return,
Whose kindness never ends.

I never could repay you
For everything, you see -
You probably think it's nothing,
But it means the world to me!

Life's so full of ups and downs,
We don't know what to do,
But just to make it smoother is -
A special friend like you!

*K N Fordham*

## Mum

Mum is the one
who's love shines through,
in all the things
we find to do.

When good or bad,
she forgives it all.
As she sees only love
to give to all.

She's there to mend
our broken hearts,
to keep us from harm,
in the dark.

Her love never fails
and never ends.
She's the one we love
until the end.

*Sylvia E Clark*

## MY MEMORIES

At ninety-two years of age, I still hold fast
To family ties, and memories of the past,
To my parents, for memorable childhood days,
Making my life happy in so many different ways.

To my beloved husband, with whom, down through the years,
I shared many hours of pleasure, laughter and tears,
Life wasn't easy, but we faced problems together.
Love and determination helping us hard times to weather.

To my dear son, whose birth gave us so much pleasure,
And as he grew older, many memories to treasure,
Visiting him in Ethiopia, where he was improving the nation's grain,
Hoping in future to prevent national starvation again.

Staying overnight at Rift Valley Game Park, where I saw,
Many rare animals and exotic birds galore
Invited to British Embassy's garden party for Armistice Day,
In palatial surroundings all colourful and gay.

Taking me to USA a 4,500 mile tour, so much to see and recall,
Yellowstone Park, with hot geysers, like 'Old Faithful' 100 ft tall,
Via Wyoming, the Grand Tetons, Salt Lake City, arriving at night,
To view setting sun on Grand Canyon, an unforgettable sight.

My two lovely grandchildren, watching their progress,
And now their families, wishing them every success,
Nothing can dim happy memories, thank you all once again,
I am so very grateful, they will always remain.

*E Kathleen Jones*

## YOU'RE MY FRIEND

You're my friend
And I've come to miss you when you're not here
You sit beside me
And all my sadness disappears
You have your world
And it's so far removed from mine
Yet your love sends forth its feelers
With which my own heart do entwine

Too many times
Words stay unspoken which should be said
We fear the outcome
Should our hearts lose their dread
And let emotions
That for so long have lain concealed
Burst out into the open
And let our illicit love be revealed

Yes you're my friend
And so forever I must love from afar
I have no right
Your present life to mar
So stay my friend
And I'll dream of how my world would be
Should there ever come a time
When you and I were free.

*Don Woods*

## HOME AND AWAY

My adult son with special needs
Left home because I'm unable now to care
He now trusts in others
It's lovely and only fair.

He lives in a place
Full of warmth and love
It's full of happiness
Like heaven above.

He has many friends
People who support and care
An extended family of sisters and brothers
Expresses his feeling of wanting to be there.

They're a band of unsung heroes
Who fill his life with so much TLC
I'm glad he's there
Now he can't be with me.

*Ann Weavers*

## SIGHTS, SOUNDS AND SMELLS OF CHRISTMAS PAST

Hysterical outbursts, peels of laughter.
Repetition of question and answers.
Mum's good humour enforced by elasticised patience.
Brothers and sisters robustly competing.
Suspended laughter as balloons burst.
Fear of retribution, Mum nods.
Seasonal treasures emerge from hibernation.
Knowingly a Jacob's biscuit tin with a paper wrapper reappears.
Contents secured in old newspapers.
From a disused pillowcase colourful paper chains
And sparkling tinsel strands.
Finally a huge harlequin paper bell,
Willing held together using dress pins.
Seasonal adornment for the kitchen window,
Framed by a rectangular white surrounding.
Christmas cards displayed on thread clothes lines, festoon the walls.
A nativity scene complements the festive décor.
Stones and sand filled wooden box waits patiently in the parlour.
Dad, Christmas tree, and broken biscuits return from market.
Courageously a turf and stick fire struggles against the odds.
Many hands dress the tree in traditional seasonal regalia.
Pantry played host to an abundance of edible wealth.
Christmas cake, white icing soft to the touch.
Breadcrumbs, currents, spices, eggs, sugar and butter stood to attention.
Two large saucepans plod together in unison, steaming plum puddings.
Tantalising aromas composedly explode.
Scullery table was reserved for the turkey,
Plucked and synched with mentholated spirits.
Underneath two white enamel buckets held vegetable and potatoes,
Eagerly awaiting, engagement on Christmas Day.

*Linda White*

## PARENTAL LOVE

Selfish love abounds,
Enveloping and enmeshing man,
In a heady embrace.

Its measured kisses,
Oozing with honied promise,
Are cheaply harvested;
Leaving the bitter taste
Of disillusionment.

But selfless love survives,
Manifesting itself in parental love.
Its essential essence
Is the continually rediscovered
Yet ever present force;
Which is unassuming
And unfaltering.

It gives without counting the cost,
Yet remains beyond price;
Spiritual and infinite,
A divine gift.

*D J Fenwick*

# REFLECTIONS

Christmas Day now over, the children fast asleep,
the snow outside is falling almost ankle deep.

Grandpa's watching TV, in his favourite chair,
nursing private sadness as Grandma can't be there.

Dad's asleep exhausted, prostrate on new settee,
I'm off to the kitchen still no rest for me.

The kitchen looks untidy, in a Christmas way,
all the food and wrapping that comes with Christmas Day.

Piles of teatime dishes, need to clean and stack,
In the new dishwasher, rack by rack by rack.

Christmas hats and crackers, now to throw away,
remnants of the fun we had this Christmas Day.

Turkey, ham and salad, to cover in food wrap,
house cat waiting at the door for my vacant lap.

Won't be long I tell her, then we can also rest,
in contented family fashion, Christmas night is best.

Home filled with love and warmth, of a day well spent,
reflections of this special day and all it really meant.

Memories of childhood, and bulging stockings on the bed,
mixture of emotions now going round and round in my head.

All the things my mum did, although could not afford,
to see that Father Christmas for 'good children' did reward.

The excitement of those long off days, are with me through the years,
and Christmas night brings memories and sometimes private tears.

Dad is lost without her, but safe in the family fold,
Christmas is emotional in more ways when we're old.

Clearing in the kitchen, the chore we used to share,
it's hard this Christmas night to know you're never there.

I feel your love around me, and know your gentle way,
and missed you more than ever throughout this Christmas Day.

***Denny***

## LOVING SISTERS' TOGETHERNESS

Four years between three sisters; we are close,
When we're together chatter is jocose,
Times separated, keep in touch by phone,
Dearly love each other, not voiced but shown,
Went about together; wartime children,
In blitz frightened of being left orphans.

Bombed out, survived, few minor injuries,
Just new 'teens' flustered by our fripperies;
'Bras' and briefs hanging, strung from window frame
Remains, house front lit by gas main aflame;
Than demolished home, left without abode,
Age when undies, sex, subjects sealed, vetoed.

Saturday nights danced, live band, 'til midnight,
Walked home, no transport, arrived at dawn light,
If heard chatting to boys we met, outside,
'Late!' called parents, 'Say goodnight, then inside!'
Morn, Mum sat on bed discussed dance 'til noon
Who were there? Old and new? Any harpooned?
Joyful, together, happy and single,
'No sex girls!' Vowed! Impressed mental jingle.

War ended, division, weddings, children,
'Sister' dates consumed to oblivion,
Some counties between our residences,
Agreed, aged parents must take precedence.

Helped one sister thro' two family deaths
It's her time now to renew life, draw breath,
Broods have flown nests, sisters three, meet sometimes,
Chat, laughter rings again as in past times,
Years vanish to our springtime, new peacetime,
Regain youth pre-launch of life's pantomime.

*Hilary Jill Robson*

## A Tribute To My Mum

I'll never underestimate everything you've done
From the day you conceived me making you my mum
You've always been there to lend a hand
To lead me to the promised land
You've been a mother and a friend
Someone there for me to depend
Someone to look upon with pride
Memories that I find hard to hide
A mum in a million, one to treasure
A tribute to you Mum, with all my pleasure.

*Dawn Moore*

## CIRCLE OF LOVE

Linked like a ringed chain
No beginning, no end
And every link is equal
In its loop and bend

Strong in construction
Bonded in force
Measured in truth
Family of course!

Here, dwells love
Patience and care
Kindness, compassion
Virtues so rare

Here, no deception
No resentment dwells
No rivalling siblings
In trivial hells

For where love exists
The ego does not
So true family ties
Are knotted a lot

And true family builds
Constructing the truth
Destroying the false
And all things uncouth

For in this domain
Of unity's tryst
No form of division
Could ever exist.

*Gemini Cherry*

## FAMILY CRIES...

Does he love me? Or not!
   He loves me? Does he care?
What-not, we ain't got
   Have we, a lot t'share?
And, care we did, long time ago
   But now, what have we, t'show?

I love her, tho' it hurts
   Bad, when she was puttin' me down;
And there don't seem no 'concert'
   Between us: just a frown
Covering the Sunday dinner...
   They call me 'the' sinner!

Winner, am I? Tho' I, always lose,
   N'confusing, it is this 'play'
On words n' hearts that confuse
   Us all, in the true way;
And only Christ can heal our woes
   Stop the treading, on our toes!

Does she love him? Do I know
   What goes on in the family mind?
N' the flow of bad vibes make me wanna go
   And spend time, with someone that's kind:
But, for all that, I shall remain
   In their hands, tho' they think I'm insane!

We shall love in Him: and (that's) the test
   To trust, in God, for the best
And rest, in the fact that He, shall win
   And bring His balm midst the 'din'
Of confusing relationships that remain
   T'be mended, when the good Lord, He deign!

*Anon*

## NEIL

My shining star
who came to me
not in a car
sat nearby
at a party do
oozing with love
through and through.
what a lucky girl?
I must be
to meet someone
so special,
alas for me.

*Kristina Howells*

## WHO GAVE YOU THAT SMILE?

I can recall so clearly
The first time that we met;
He thought his chat up line was so cool.
'Say, who gave you that smile?'
I'd heard it before in some old film
But somehow it never failed.

We married too young after
An innocent romance,
Now he's no more than a stranger.
Lying in a hospital bed
Listening to that awful 'beep beep' sound.
I know that I look a mess
But if you can't see me there isn't any point,
I don't want to sparkle for anyone but you.

I didn't notice when the machine stopped
My heart was beating far too loud.
I think back to all the times our families
Said that it would never last.
I guess that this has proved right,
But by God we put up a fight;
Because you gave me that smile.

*Vicky Stevens*

## YEAR ON

Hours spent in washing clothes
A look for this, need more than clothes
Pass on the hint, the time is close
Pray everything not charred, like toast
Yoke, round neck, when case's closed

How far is it, will tide be in
Oh Mum, is it true you cannot swim
Look, harbour light past yonder hill
Is Dad awake, he'll miss the thrill
Did you pack my favourite thing?
A new day came, sun lit the sky
Yes, let's hope days do not fly.

*Geof Farrar*

## LOVING FEELING

Why is it the ones we love
Seem to be sent from up above,
When we worry and feeling uptight,
They say the things that seems so right,
When we're going out of our minds with anxiety,
They'll put you right back up there in society.
Those deep emotional thoughts run wild,
Feeling like a desperately seeking child,
And so you need a shoulder to cry,
Which is where a loved one will lie,
Feeling insecure and wanting to hide,
They'll welcome you with arms open wide,
When you don't know what's so wrong,
Their love can be so rewardly strong,
That's why we need family and a friend,
Cos they'll be there whatever . . . 'til the end.

*Nichole Jackman*

## PUSHKA
*(Cat Of The 60s)*

The small round ball of fluff was singed, a red hot
coal had fallen from the fire, when I saw this I cringed.

My cousins gave the tiny cat to me,
its fur grew white the way that it should be.

A mottled coat of black and white with grey,
she ate scraps from our table every day.

I had a watch which had a nice chrome strap,
she played with it as she lay on my lap.

When I had taken it off for the night,
it disappeared before the morning light.

I rode my cycle off to work by our old house clock's time,
and wondered how Pushka had worked out how to do the crime.

Later when I married my cat she came to stay,
but, I lived with my husband's folk and they put her away.

Pushka, she had two kittens so, they said we'll just keep those,
my husband took his rifle and said 'this is the kindest way,
that a beast can seek repose.'

Although I did not like it I knew we could not keep all three,
I had a young child also, thus no chance to disagree.

Later on I learned that he and his psychopathic mate,
had vied to strangle my best friend, she'd had an awful fate.

My husband may be dead and gone but, I still think of that,
I'll never keep a pet again, especially not a cat.

*Jean Paisley*

## FROM ONE SHILLING AND THREE PENCE A WEEK

Mountaineers are we from birth,
O'er infinite heights of earth.
Grandpa Taylor eight years old,
Wakened at five in the cold,
To work in the cotton mill.
Pauper still.

At eighteen coached in God's word,
His prayer 'Set us free O Lord,
Help us to reach the highest;
Our Master calls to conquest,
Gladly we heed and obey
Everyday.'

Mother Carol's gracious love,
Shines in glory from above.
Cheerful Jeanette's gentle rays,
Fill our hearts with joyous praise.
Their heaven-born faith prevails.
Distrust fails.

World-wide our family-fold,
Far east, deep south, friends enrolled.
Phone and mail to distant place,
Spread beams of care o'er sea's face.
One in heart life's richest store,
Evermore.

Kinsfolk climb upwards with might,
Till glimmers of hope are in sight.
Truth's blest fellowship boundless,
Leads to victory endless.
Centred in our Leader's host,
Uppermost.

*James Leonard Clough*

## SOMEONE WHO MEANS THE WORLD TO ME

That special someone is you Mum,
not just to me but to everyone,
your kids, family and friends,
people that love to beg, borrow and lend
and those that see you with money and feel,
they have to help you spend.

You give even when you don't have,
help others so often and don't get any thanks,
you would rather give than borrow,
can see when people are suffering in sorrow,
if you don't have,
you would rather do without.

When people need help
they automatically think let's give (Sharon)
(Aunty Sharon) a shout!
When you're suffering you still provide for us,
without making a big fuss.

You are a good person,
if you don't see it, everyone else does,
it's people like you that God really loves.

When you are broke no one will know,
you still get on with life so it don't show,
some day you will get your reward,
so continue with God's blessings and, wait on the 'Lord'.

**Shantel Faure  (17)**

## I Almost Didn't Have A Mum

I almost didn't have a mum
When she lay sick in a hospital bed
A nasty tumour was the trouble
Worse of all, it was in her head

She had a series of dangerous ops
In Oxford and became very ill
She caught infections and developed diabetes
She's allergic to a lot of things as well

It is amazing that she survived
She is a determined and brave lady
She wasn't going to die yet
To her it wasn't even a maybe

When she became fifty
A birthday we thought she wouldn't see
We pulled out all the stops
And made a fuss of this brave lady

She is still going to work now
And can use a computer as well
This very determined person shows
You can survive things as my poem tells.

*P Edwards*

## FATHER OF THE FATHERLESS

I have no earthly father,
my mother ran away.
No sisters or brothers
to talk with, or play.
Abandoned by the roadside,
I beg for food to live,
the world just passes by,
too busy to love or give.
But I have someone else
who reaches down with love.
And he takes care of me -
He's my Father - up above.

*Ken Price*

## Helen Remembered

You were a shining light to all who knew you.
Racked with ill health and almost blind,
Housebound for many years,
You never moaned or grumbled,
Railed against your lot.
You loved your God and lived your life
For others not for self.
Many there were who came to visit you,
Burdened by worries,
Often in ill health.
A brief time in your company
And they forgot their grievances and woes,
Their spirits were uplifted,
Your example gave them hope.
They went away
Refreshed, renewed.
No longer are you with us
But you live within our hearts,
Memories of you will never fade,
You touched our lives,
You still remain
A comfort in life's trials.
My thanks to God, I give,
For your outgoing life,
Your love and friendship given without stint,
A truly great example of God's love,
His servant here on earth.

*Roma Davies*

## CHRISTMAS REFLECTIONS

Christmas came and quickly went,
And all our pennies have been spent.
All the lights that brightly shone,
And turkey carcasses have gone.

We worked and worked a complete year,
For several hours of Christmas cheer.
And soon before we know what's what,
We'll hear, 'What Christmas pressies, have you got?'

For it will soon be back again,
To cause once more, financial drain.
But this time I'll no longer lie,
I'll tell them of the son on high.

And of the Claus I'll tell them this,
A postman who brings children bliss.
A messenger of God and Son,
To celebrate the chosen one.

*Geoffrey Woodhead*

## A SPECIAL TREE

We have a very big fine tree,
and it has grown for all to see.
For it starts from the very top,
and it's growth will never stop.

All the branches are very sound,
and its main roots are off the ground.
From each branch several buds show,
They too start to flower and grow.

Over the years it's grown so big,
at first it was just a little twig.
Even today we try to trace
Branches that maybe a different race.

Years and years this tree goes back
Sometimes you think you're loosing track.
As here and there, the branches seem still,
Often a place one cannot fill.

But as this tree starts to expand,
Branches maybe found in a different land.
For this tree will never come to an end,
Because its buds the branches will defend.

*Margaret Upson*

## NANA'S STATION

I love to catch the train sometimes
Nana lives just up the line
We have to stop
At strange old stations
Twelve until our destination
Nana's station is so neat
With flower pots
All bright complete
Everything is painted bright
It really is a pretty sight
We get there in no time at all
Nana's waiting she's quite small
Can't wait until I hug her tight
Wonder what's for tea tonight.

*Jeanette Gaffney*

## MAYFLOWER'S CHILDREN

On the high seas they made for the New World
brave Pilgrims - just a handful of humanity
with the hope of God in their hearts.
On that epic voyage
Elizabeth Hopkins gave birth to Oceanus,
a son for Stephen, another brother for Giles.

Her birth pangs were at one
with the creaking timber of the heaving ship
bearing in turn its own labour pain;
the strain and crack of mighty oak
against that vaster amniotic fluid.
The cry of anguish as her red tide flowed
and the echo of a tentative cry
as tiny lungs now filled with an intake
of the air that far above them
gave life to the wide white deep-breathing sails.

And when weeks later from the great ship's womb
they were birthed onto an unknown and hostile shore
like latter-day Jonahs,
winter waited patiently
hunger hovered near
and deprivation dealt its death blows.
Half their number dead - just three score spared!

Yet still they hoped and loved,
built and planted, mourned and celebrated
founding their colony, an indomitable people.

Tenth, eleventh and twelfth generations
we gathered at Christmas
to celebrate family and a Saviour's birth.

*Patricia Hopkins*

## VALENTINE REVISITED

Thou wretched muse of human time
Who tolls the days and keeps the hour
That robbed so many years of valentine
And kept me locked within thy power.

Whilst I like Orpheus travelled wide
And dreamed of passion's promised land
Slipped helplessly down the slippery slide
Propelled by nature's treacherous hand.

The barren years locked in a heart
That loved a love unfound
No practice at the lover's art
This muse so cruel all hopes confound.

Yet suddenly the sun appears
As if by magic up above
Banishing all the doubts and fears
For I had found my life long love.

*C O Burnell*

## PEACE

Imagine the world full of warmth and peace
The thought of hope that will never cease
Religion irrelevant as united we stand
Terrorism outlawed and hate is banned

What does it matter our ethnic group
Different cultures each bear a fruit
A fruit, a spirit, the symbol of life
To live in harmony without no strife

Political leaders what's gone wrong
The sea of tranquillity for what we long
Different countries with a different passion
People are starving with food they ration

Why are we not joined in congregation
To heal the world and find salvation
To forget and forgive within our heart
A new target needed for this to start

Banish the thoughts of disruption and despair
The world is crying yet we can repair
Repair our souls and heal the mind
That is the dream I'm trying to find.

*John Lee*

## MELLOW YELLOW

Beside our dog, on the ground,
Our cockatiel, could be found,
Flying free every night,
She enjoyed an evening flight,
Feathers of daffodil yellow and white,
She was a cheeky cockatiel,
Our dog, we can reveal,
Had to share, her chew bone,
From our dog never a moan,
Mostly birds, a dog hates!
But these two, were best mates!
Our feathered pet, did look frail,
We found a lump, on her tail.
Six months later, she was sick,
Our pet's end, did come quick.

She was a very pretty bird,
To call her 'Oscar' was absurd,
We thought she, was a he!
Soon finding it could not be,
Once, putting up the Christmas tree,
We found eggs, that totalled three!
In our garden one fir tree,
Marks her resting place to be,
When daffodils, flutter in a breeze
Her yellow feathers, were like these,
Now daffodils, to us reveal,
Fond memories of a cockatiel.

**Sheila Walters**

## WHAT'S HAPPENED

What kind of questions
should we ask
to rectify the times past
there isn't such a big divide
and poor people do not starve
fundamentally the shame
of being poor
is being eradicated for sure
but what of greed
and people cheating
and principles being swallowed up.
It seems that effluence
has done nothing for honesty,
in this modern world today
principles have gone astray,
so how do we define riches?

*Mary Tickle*

## TO LOVE

Dreaming
like a
rose
asleep
or sighing
'neath
the moon
love
utters
forth
a
sentence
sweet
soon
my
darling
soon.

*David A Bray*

## THE VIOLIN

It was standing in a window, a lovely looking thing
Dark and brown and shiny, a lovely violin
I bought it for £300, a bargain, so I'm told.
Taking out my money, just enough, so it was sold.
I booked myself some lessons for music every week.
Every time I practised it made a funny squeak.
People all around me seem to disappear every time I play it
So displeasing to the ear
When I played it at a concert
Everybody laughed especially when so nervous
One felt a fool, not half
I passed exams, had certificates to prove,
I just scraped through
My hands just shook like jelly
The examiner said, 'You'll do!'
So now I just go busking to help the charities
It gets a little money, the needy are so pleased
To think that we will help them and give them our support.
I'm glad I bought a violin, but still not playing as I ought?
I'm now playing as I ought?

*Carole Andrews*

## THE BEST THINGS IN LIFE IS I'M DIFFERENT

We can't be who you want us to be
We are all different in our hearts, body and soul.
We can't be who we're not.
God made us to be who we are today,
Sorry if you don't like the colour of skin,
But I'm different
We can't be all the same cause we're different,
You tell us to be more like this person, but why?
Is it because I'm different

It doesn't matter about the way I look
Or about the colour of our skin or the size we are
Big or small it doesn't matter.
We are all different in many ways
And that's the best thing in life.

*Kezian Martin*

## MY HOPE

When I go from here,
I want to leave behind me,
A world that will be richer
for the experience of having known me.
I want the children, my friends, animals and birds
to be a little less afraid of human beings,
because they have known me.
For I have cared for them and loved them.
And far from doing them any harm, in some small way
I have done them good.
I want to leave the trees I have planted,
rustling with my thoughts.
Trees that have heard me speaking to them
when we were alone together.
Trees that one day
long after I have disappeared in body form
will still in some mysterious way
cherish their secret knowledge of knowing me.
Then others who shelter from the rain,
or seek shade under their branches
shall catch the peace that went out of me.
I want to store up riches in the wind.
Leave blessings travelling upwards to the stars,
I want the many tears I have shed,
to come again in the dew,
I want to leave the children and nature
richer for having known me.

*Patricia M Farbrother*

## HOGMANAY TIME

Midnight . . .
Big Ben strikes twelve.
Anticipation for one second past,

Second, seconds and minute . . .

Resolutions, new start, new ideas, hope,
Last year, depressed, sad and lonely,
People came and went.

Second, seconds and minute,
Minute, minutes and hour . . .

Champagne-intoxication,
Dance and noise,
The Hogmanay party and
Auld Lang Syne,

Second, seconds and minute,
Minute, minutes and hour,
Hour, hours and day . . .

New day, new year,
New wars,
New resolutions broken,
New crimes committed,
New mistakes made,
New hatred bred . . .
Same old me.

Year, months, month,
Month, weeks, week.
Week, days, day . . . day . . . day
After
Day
Same
Old
Day . . .
Happy New Year.

*Humera Hanif*

## YOU

A curtain of hair fell over your face,
Those yesterday eyes held a shadowy trace,
Then a smile just escaped like a dog in a chase . . .
I saw you today.

Is love a question?
Do feelings erupt
Like cathedral bells chiming
On a hot sunburnt day?
With nothing to do
But lie back on the hay staring at blue?
And I'm alone now
Just thinking of you,
I saw you today.

Do you know that you're lovely,
Has she told you that yet?
Does she love you for nothing,
Or haven't you met?
It's raining outside
In that soft summer way . . .
In one moment of time
I saw you today.

*Jane Isaac*

## MY HEART'S DESIRE

My heart's desire for you
And for you alone my friend.
Together we shall comfort
Each other to life end.
For when I'm far away from you,
I miss the comfort of your heart.
But with our two hearts joined together
We know that we shall never part.

*J Hickman*

## BLIND DATE

This Venus floated towards me
Shimmering in an illusionist aura.
Her silver halo bedazzled my invading thoughts -
And expectations from this rendezvous -
My aspirations reached heights not aspired to before.
In the end - we moulded together
Like two tributaries flowing separately,
Then finally becoming as one
We flowed into the night!

*B R Walker*

## FRIENDS

These most of us have many kinds,
Some with very intellectual minds,
Our friends we choose,
And wouldn't want to lose.

They share in our troubles and joy,
We also have moments when they annoy,
True friendship stays the course,
Loyalty is also very staunch.

People have friends all over England,
Many writing letters by hand,
Some we are in reach and often see,
To have friends how happy it can be.

*Pamela Earl*

## HERS

I saw a little child the other day
Was fascinated as I watched her play
She had set the table and was offering tea
To all her friends imaginary
She was talking, they apparently answering back
Only she understood this one way chat.
She had some dolls, and her favourite ted
An old fashioned cradle and a bed,
A toy dog was there and a cat
There was a piece of material for a mat
This was her land of fantasy
It was a pleasure for me to see
This was hers, a happy mood
One in which I could not intrude.

*Gladys C'Ailceta*

## Dark Nights

I'm in my room all alone it's so creepy and really dark
There's no noise it's really quiet you'd probably be
able to hear an ant walk.
I am alone and really scared
But there's no one here to even care.
Suddenly I hear a noise it makes me jump and very alert
Stood there is a frightening creature all covered in dirt.
What do you want and why are you here is what I say
But the creature just looks and walks away.
I beg him to leave this is not where he belongs
But he roughly replies it's me who is wrong.
The creature then hands me a list telling me he can't tell me anymore
He then leaves through a crack in the door.
The following morning I wake to find it was all a dream
And then I see not all is what it seems.
The list the monster gave to me was on my bed
Sitting there waiting to be read.
I go and get it and start to read
Then I see that this creature was hurt and needed me.
It was a man under a curse
His life was bad and couldn't get any worse.
He needed to fall in love and for this love to be returned
He says in the list he wanted to learn
How to be kind and loving like before the spell
I didn't know and I treated him unwell.
Now I will never be able to help him now
But then who is this yes I am right we have been
given a second chance show how
We could love each other and get rid of this bad curse
And be together for better or worse.

*Lisa Keevan*

## DREAMING OUT OF THE WINDOW

Dreaming out of the window
Sailing away and away
How can he expect me to face the front
On such a beautiful day?
Boy, yes you boy! Pay attention boy!
Yes, you there!
You with the gormless look on your face
Have you been listening to a single thing
I've been saying?
I really don't know why I bother wasting
My breath on silly little morons like you
It's not as if you're going to do anything
With your miserable little lives - anyway -
All you're really good for is -
Dreaming out of that damn window
Flying away on the wings of a dream -
So beautiful, no power on earth
Could prevent me from squeezing
Through the bars of mediocrity
And sailing away on a wave of
Pure tranquillity!
Dreaming out of the window
Sailing away and away
How can he expect me to face the front
On such a beautiful day?

*Rod Trott*

### SHIVA'S LOVE SONG (FOR W H AUDEN AND T)

Start all the clocks
Unzip the moon

Release a cloud of red balloons

Start all the clocks
Unpack the sun

Abandon sadness
Feeling glum

I am no longer on my own
The dog had found a brand new bone

She is my morning noon and night
The compass points of my delight

She is my angel of the east
Her train a skein of snow white geese

The winds twelve quarters I have found
My princess from a golden town

So everything will now get better
Like rainbows after stormy weather

And I am floating like a kite
Upon the winds of my delight.

**Richard Bonfield**

## MEMORIES IN THE SKY

That blanket, big woollen and grey,
Under which, as a child, I'd slept.
Lay, I spy now, dormant in the sky.
Hovering over homes and gardens,
Slowly passing by.

Amongst the clouds white; so white,
As my ceiling and door,
Around the bedroom skirting board.
The room in which I once played,
The sky to me, kindly, replays.
The memory that youth somehow decayed.

Stressless blue sky. I recall my playtime.
Up and then down the street on scooters,
My brother and I.
Indoors, many times, a game of Star Wars.
At bedtime we'd chatter away and continue to play.
Until our eyes gave way to gravities laws.

In the darkening sky I see
The joy. The happiness I've left behind me.
My childhood in the sky.
Who else is watching my memories but I.
Blackening sky that remembers my play,
Please leave behind this memory for a keepsake
Or return it to me again some day.

*Richard Turland*

## INSIGNIFICANCE

When you look at all the stars in the sky.
And think they go on for a billion miles.
*Cos I do.*
If you think about the insect world.
Millions of them to each one of us.
*Yes it is true.*

The way we think is arrogant.
Our thoughts are solid like cement.
We believe in equality.
Only if it suits individually.
*What a shame . . .*

We are like an insect.
Where nobody is perfect.
Everyone is worth it.

If we substitute our hate.
Fill the earth with love.
Put down our self destruct mode
And follow a more peaceful code
Since, man's folly is his own.
For the Gods have all gone home
They've left us to our plight,
To destroy earth with this spite.
From petty, insecure things,
The fact is it's all over when you die.

So look out to outer space,
*And concentrate*
On getting into that 'other' place.
Let's start to build a better world,
For the sake of little boys and girls.

***A Norton***

## THE PRESENTS

The present we gave mother
Exploded on her face
She smiled and said, how lovely
The cat left in great haste

To get outside, somewhere to hide
Before we went in case

The deftest kick
Might lay on thick
Her present's out of place

The present for my dearest
Was received as a cloud
From overhead fell on the bed
And hid her like a shroud

It's lovely, said my darling
The hinges on my tomb
Began to squeak,
As the lid creaked and
Came down with a boom

I'm better off receiving
Then going to the store
Don't have to leave when I receive
I buy, I'm shown the door

One wonders if the same is true
With people who are poor
Or if they
Simply smile and say,
It's lovely -anymore?

*Peter Asher*

## FATHER'S DAY

Dad can you recollect the day,
That you and I went to our first football match,
The time you also took me fishing, when it was cold,
And we caught a big one, which nearly pulled me in,

Without you there that day to help me out,
No fish, would have been had for tea
But oh, what a whopper it was, I also remember
Not knowing what sort it was, and neither did you,

But it's teeth were sharp and many, thought I had a problem,
Come to think of it now, it was ugly as well,
But once you have cooked it to perfection
As you always do, by heck, it's taste was mouth-watering

Well, this is your special day, but once a year
So I am sending you my best wishes in your direction
Hoping you have a really great day
For I still remember you, and the things we did

As you are my father, which is one in a million
I gave a big thank you, for being you, and there for me,
Whenever I needed help, and a shoulder to cry on
My Father, the best in the world, wasn't far away.

*S J Davidson*

## It's A New Dawn

I sat and thought today
What kind of childhood did I have
Could I remember, No
I guess I'm getting older?

As I look out of my window
I see the frost upon the trees
Little birds searching for food
I guess I live today.

Getting old is not my option
Living now is all I ask
To see the birds upon the trees
See seasons come and go.

The only sure thing, about this life
Is that we come and go
We bide our time upon this earth
Making history as we go.

**Carole A Cleverdon**

## HUNTING HOLLY

I took off a walking into the long wintry woods
every tree was solid and dashing with its sprinkling icy coat
pathways of crusted flakes drifted out in all directions
which one would lead me to that elusive holly tree.

Each footstep broke the virgin snow
rasping treads left a trail of silent hollows
the breath blew hot and cold in a December sun
though camouflaged hands were warm the air was numbing.

Threading a thin line through bushy pine needles
I met a man with some bags that are sprouting prickly ears
he ushered my feet forward to the centre of the earth
once again these eyes frolic to a seasonal first.

Soon there are branches enriching my favourite walls
behold the royal prince of the evergreen world
uplifting the spirits to rekindle that festive mood
a treasured gift from the heart of the wintry woods.

*Gerard Wilson*

## MISSED

I missed the bus today, the driver saw me running,
Ignoring me with a smirk, he zoomed past anyway,
I missed the chance to say goodbye when my father died.

I missed the post at lunchtime now it is delayed,
Another day passes before you read what I had to say,
I missed the chance to say I love you on your last day.

I missed the sun this morning it sulked behind a cloud,
Reminding me of hazy days penetrating words I said,
I missed the chance to say I'm sorry selfish that was me.

I missed the rain tonight wet and cold reminiscent of tears,
I did not mean to break your heart in all those wasted years,
I missed the chance to say I cared, you washed away my fears.

I missed the twinkling stars against a black velvet sky,
Your eyes sparkled when you laughed brightness in my world,
I missed the chance to say to you dear dad you're missed.

*Helen Blackadder*

## THE HOMECOMING

In the sunshine of mid-afternoon
It's wrong to wish for night too soon.
Yet, looking at your sun bright pillow
I long to see the moonlight shimmer.

Dreaming in the golden glow
With sunbeams dancing to and fro
The hours go by with steady pace;
Oh why can not they run a race?

At last the sunset fills the sky
The evening breeze through treetops sigh.
The first star shines with silver light,
As darkness brings the longed for night.

And now I hear your car go by
And now my heart is full of joy
I hear your step upon the path
And know that you are home, at last.

*Meryl*

## THE EARTH WILL BECOME A PARADISE

Paradise in heaven is where good spirits dwell
Who have spent their life on earth well.
They shed a beneficial influence,
Evil is viewed by them with abhorrence.

Wisdom, hope, faith and charity -
Such values ennoble humanity,
High standards will reflect,
And always have a good effect.

The earth will be filled with heavenly light
Flourishing and prospering in everyone's sight,
Motives will always be positive and good,
Humanity will be fed with spiritual food.

>   Through goodness mankind will rise,
>   The earth will become a paradise.

**M MacDonald-Murray**

## THE STORM

Warning pot bellied clouds
amass for morning storm,
then dance a noisy rumba
that starts slanting squally rain.

Thunder falls as a crash of plates
from the black smudged heavens
as endless torrents cascade
into angry churning rivulets.

A million jillion raindrops
bounce from antlered oaks
with dreary syllabic rhythm
while meadows are laundry sodden.

The clouds relent their duty at dusk
allowing wind - biting enjoyment.
Snow and hail now participate -
to snuffle on distant razored hills.

*Alex Branthwaite*

## BEACHCOMBER

Beachcomber on the windy beach
the wide smile of the shore.
Shell-spangled seas
remember these
you're looking for:

Memories washed clean where soft waves lick
old hurts from melting sand
till shells, glinting
are beckoning
a childlike hand.

Grey gulls that ride the wind's broad back,
cheat grave from brutish flow
of simple air -
We can learn there
what the gulls know.

The ancient rhythm of the waves
still echoes in our breath
and changing tides
quietly confide
of passing death.

Beachcomber on the timeless beach.
The wide smile of the shore
is yours - the sea
recalls what she
was looking for!

*Chris Glassfield*

## SPRING CHICKS

On spring days as daffies grew
Busy birds did work,
Back and forth they merrily flew
Picking - prodding - dirt.

Snowdrops sprouted purest white
As nests were taking shape
Buttercups like golden lights
Chicks would soon awake.

Children ventured in the lanes,
But mother said 'Don't touch,'
Flossie ran to chase a stone,
Soon the chicks would hatch.

The cows across the field did moo,
Painfully giving birth,
Sheep would have their moment too
Daisies graced the paths.

Ducklings in the water swam
As Johnny sailed his ship,
Sally walking with her mum
While Daddy had a kip.

Riders glided through the dales,
Breezes brushing cheeks
Grandma with her mixing bowl
Busy baking cakes.

Children skip in frilly frocks,
Dancing in the corn
All dressed up with shiny locks
At last the chicks are born.

*Wendy Watkin*

## The Dawn

Everywhere is as black as pitch
Not one tiny sound can be heard
Nothing moves - the world is so still
Not even the chirp of a bird.
Suddenly there's a finger of light
It looks like a tear in the gloom.
The light breaks thru' with streaks of gold
And gradually lights up my room.
The sky's now a web of orange and gold
It brightens each leaf on the tree
Even the grass is shimmering too
Wow! All this splendour is free!
A great orange ball comes into sight
And the sky is a blaze of light
The dawn has arrived - no more night!
The scene is so beautifully bright.

*E J Sharman*

## AN CLÀRSACH
(The Celtic Harp)

Emotions
gently assailed
sound battalions
awaken
genes of time
musical heritage
clàrsach-strung
ageless
harper
plucking
my ancestral
spinal chords
aeons of reverberations'
grandeur
summoning
mind accompaniments
mellifluous vaulting
ancient melodies
airing
bardic airs
extant presence.

*Séamas M Ó Dálaigh*

## FOREVER SWEET

Through the tears
of a child
I know your heart
smiles.
When I was young
the sun was sweet.
When I'm old
the roses will sleep.

*Helen Owen*

## WAKE UP OLD FOSSIL, WAKE UP!

The winds of destiny are blowing wild
The hounds of fate, already a prey hunting.
Senses of waves and washes of pain, float
Threatening to flood and drown all human resistance
With the rapidity of red-hot lava of an active volcano.

Will you on wings of threatening storm fly
Leaving behind debris of heartache and pain?
Has absolute power-lust clouded your reason
Beyond the shadowy, impenetrable veils of time?
Do you mean all attempts at embracing change are vain?

Wake up! Old fossil, wake up! There are influences beyond,
The visible, clear, plain, underside;
Sometimes malignant, sometimes benign
Which, with surgical precision, dictate all outcomes of earthly affairs
With patience and dedication of love divine.

Wake up! Old fossil, wake up!
For winds of destiny are blowing, change
And hounds of fate, already hold a crown
To crown him king, whose heart embraces, change;
Whose mind, bathed in refreshing pools of infinite grace
Knows that the only thing constant on earth is change
And infinite wisdom, dictates the outcome of all earthly affairs.

***George Saurombe***

# SUBMISSIONS INVITED
## *SOMETHING FOR EVERYONE*

**POETRY NOW 2002** - Any subject, any style, any time.

**WOMENSWORDS 2002** - Strictly women, have your say the female way!

**STRONGWORDS 2002** - Warning! Age restriction, must be between 16-24, opinionated and have strong views. (Not for the faint-hearted)

All poems no longer than 30 lines. Always welcome! No fee! Cash Prizes to be won!

Mark your envelope (eg *Poetry Now*) **2002**
Send to:
Forward Press Ltd
Remus House, Coltsfoot Drive,
Peterborough, PE2 9JX

**OVER £10,000 POETRY PRIZES TO BE WON!**

Judging will take place in October 2002